MJ

FEED YOUR ANGEL

overcoming our addiction to ego

Hope you
enjoy the
book, which
includes
my story

:O]:

DAVID GESCHKE

:)

FEED YOUR ANGEL
overcoming your addiction to ego

David Geschke
PO Box 11
Waupun, WI 53963
(920) 382-4622

www.DavidGeschke.com
www.facebook.com/davidgeschkepage
www.twitter.com/davidgeschke
www.facebook.com/feedyourangel
www.twitter.com/feedyourangel
www.youtube.com/user/feedyourangel

Produced and printed in the United States of America.

Contents

acknowledgments

To my wife Laurie
who watched the events leading up to the publication
of this book unfold in real time.

To Kelly, Mike and Dede
who helped me change my life in an instant.

To Michael Singer and Wayne Dyer
who blazed a trail before me with their insights.

To Dave Sheffield and Alisha Wielfaert
For pushing me when I needed it.

introduction

4/9/18

I must be crazy.

Why are you writing this book? What's it about? These are the questions people asked when I told them what I was doing. Up until today, I'm not sure I've had a good answer. I'm still not sure I have a good answer, but before I begin, I want to get clear on the concept for myself if for no other reason than to avoid future awkwardness as I stumble for an appropriate answer.

As for why I'm writing this book, I got the idea to write a book called *Feed Your Angel* years ago. I held it just as a concept for a long time until one day I stumbled across an old friend of mine online. Dave "The Shef" Sheffield (www.theshef.com) had become a motivational speaker. At the time I had several different concepts for books floating around in my head, which I shared with him. He fell in love with *Feed Your Angel*. It was Dave's excitement that eventually gave this project wings.

The original idea came from talks I was giving to the recovering community. I'm a recovering alcoholic and addict with more than twenty-nine years of sobriety as of this writing. When talking to people new in their sobriety, I often used an angel-devil analogy that reflected the old cartoons and movies that showed an angel on one shoulder and a devil on the other. In those movies the depiction was usually portrayed as a fair fight—both sides equal in power. But that's not what happens in real life; one side or the other takes control. When addicts hit bottom, they have a three-hundred-pound demon on one shoulder and an angel on life support on the other. At that point you can either fight the demon—a battle you cannot win—or feed your angel. Recovery is about feeding your angel.

With Dave's excitement driving me, and using him as a mentor, I started the website www.FeedYourAngel.com, a Facebook and Twitter Page, and I began blogging. At that time, I expected to blog for a while on the subject—different ways and things you can do to feed your angel—then release the series of blogs as a book. I attended a writer's workshop and printed seventy copies of a "preview" edition. Everything was rolling right along.

Then I stopped.

Looking back, I'm not exactly sure of the order of events that killed the process, but the process did end. I presented a talk that I didn't prepare well for, and that sucked some of the life out. My day job took more and more of my time. Dave and I stopped communicating, and without his excitement and drive, I let the book project wane. For years.

I also read Nancy Levin's book *Jump – And Your Life Will Appear* at that time, and I realized that I didn't want my book to be a series of blog posts. Right out of the gate, she shares extremely personal information in her book, and I began thinking that my book should have a different format. I thought I should scrap everything I had already written and start from scratch. That also pulled a lot of wind out of my sails.

I kept the website and social media pages online, but other than an article I wrote in 2014 for a local publication, I didn't have much to report. No work was being done. People would ask how the book was coming along, and my usual answer was, "It isn't."

Fast forward to 2017 when another friend of mine Alisha Wielfaert (www.yokeandabundance.com) had become a life coach at an extremely challenging time in my life. We started looking at things and discussing a couple ideas I had shelved for years, including a four-part speaker series, which is now available on YouTube at www.youtube.com/user/feedyourangel, and writing the book you now holds in your hands today.

With Alisha's help I had decided once and for all "I'm writing this book." Because I felt compelled to do so. Not because I thought I had any answers. I'm struggling just like you are. What follows within these pages are the issues I grapple with and the ways I try to cope with them as best I can without letting darkness back in my heart.

Working with Alisha, I decided to take three weeks off and go to Florida to write *Feed Your Angel*. I wanted to be close to the Temple of the Universe (www.tou.org). Michael Singer (www.untetheredsoul.com) created the Temple and is my favorite current author. His books, *The Untethered Soul* and *The Surrender Experiment*, are fantastic. He speaks several times a week at the Temple, and I look to him for inspiration. Another big influence of mine, Wayne Dyer (www.drwaynedyer.com), also traveled to Florida and took two weeks to write his first book *Your Erroneous Zones*. I made a plan to finish and publish this book in 2018. This is, of course, the book you now hold in your hands.

Why am I writing this book? Because I got the idea to write it years ago, and that thought never went away. Too often in life we ignore the messages we receive as being unrealistic, silly, and/or frivolous. Not this one. I do believe I'm more of a transmitter here—that I will transmit the words that have already been written. But I'm compelled to see this through. And it is my intention to do so.

As for what is this book about? ... It's about trying to find peace in a life fraught with anxiety and tension. Becoming calm. Taming the ego. Finding ways to let God and love rule your heart. What follows is by no means a manual for success in these areas. I expect it to be more like me asking you to "take a walk with me here, and let's try to figure this out together."

I thank you from the bottom of my heart for your interest. I thank you for getting this far.

God is calm.

Love is open.

Come with me. Let's walk together…

David Geschke
Horsepower Farms "Treehouse"
High Springs, Florida
April 9, 2018

CHAPTER 1

my story

4/9/18 & 4/10/18

I GREW UP ON THE NORTH SIDE OF OSHKOSH, WI, a town of about fifty thousand people in the 1960s and '70s. A nice middle-class neighborhood. My father had a decent job with a manufacturing firm and an old-school German work ethic. He worked for one company basically his whole life—forty-two years at one place. You don't often see that anymore. My mother was mostly a stay-at-home mom, but she also worked at times as a bookkeeper and/or a proofreader. I was always a good student and never even thought about trying to break the rules or get away with anything. I was pretty much on the straight and narrow.

Sometime around 1972 my father was let go from the job he'd worked at for forty-two years. He was sixty-one years old, and my mom was fifty-seven at the time. I was thirteen; they had me late in life. Because of his age, he couldn't find work in his preferred field. Because of the way he was let go, he didn't receive a full pension. To this day, I remember it was a ridiculously small amount—in the vicinity of $7 to $9 a month, paid quarterly. You didn't want to see him on the day he got those checks—$9 a month for forty-two years of service? That bothered him so much that he became negative and cynical toward the end of his life. My father was a man who probably would have worked until the day he died if given the choice.

At the time Dad was let go, the business he had worked for was letting go of many employees, so he partnered with another guy who was also released and opened a liquor store—GM Beverage. Ironically, I don't remember or even think of my dad as a heavy drinker. While he certainly enjoyed alcohol, I can remember seeing him drunk only a handful of times when I was growing up. He could be a bit of a mean drinker, though.

Shortly thereafter, we sold our house and moved to the south side of town. New school. New friends. Lasted close to two years before the liquor store partnership dissolved, the business closed, and we moved back to the north side. Dad had basically retired at that point, aside from periodic odd jobs.

By then, in 1974, I was entering my first year of high school. On day one, the school assembled all the kids who had transferred from out of the district. I got to know a few of the other kids in that group and got invited to one of their houses. We listened to music, partied—whatever fourteen-year-old boys did at that time. Then much to my surprise, they started smoking marijuana. I was shocked and scared. I had absolutely no interest in that. On the spot, I made up a lie about being allergic to marijuana to get out of smoking it. I stuck with the allergy story for as long as I could, but I kept hanging out with those guys, so I eventually tried it. And, wow, I loved it.

I started smoking pot when I was fourteen years old. About the same time, I also started drinking. The minimum drinking age at that time was eighteen, and alcohol was fairly easy to get. Pot was even easier to get from the kids dealing it at the high school. Going forward, 1974 was a year that determined many things for me.

The year before, when I was still on the south side, I had told a friend of mine that I was a bass player. Why, I'll never know. Truth was I hadn't even seen a bass guitar at the time, much less tried to play one. My father was a talented singer and multi-instrumentalist, so I did inherit from him a natural musical ability. One day, this south side friend called. He had a band, their bass player just quit, and did I want the gig? I said, "Sure!" and bought myself a $20 Kingston model bass, which I played through my stereo. That was my first set up. My friend came over to my house and showed me the songs. I could actually play bass on day one, even though I had never played before. We were fourteen at the time, the songs were fairly easy, but I'll never forget my shock that I was able to do it. He never knew I had lied, and the next day we practiced with a drummer. We were terrible, but I was hooked. I started practicing two hours every day and jamming with all the local musicians. Our house became the hangout, and my parents let us practice in the basement. We drank and smoked pot and jammed all through my high school years.

Alcohol and pot soon turned into other drugs—speed, downers, acid, and whatever else I could get that was mood altering. And it all started when I was fourteen.

LSD was an amazing yet scary drug. It was not like any other drug. Depending on which variant you got—wow—you could experience hours of non-stop hallucinations. And you couldn't pull out of it once you took it. You were in for the duration. We would usually plan our acid trips because you had to be in the right frame of mind. No one wanted a bad acid trip. In 1977, I had one. I had been tripping all day with a friend of mine, and I wanted to continue, so I took a bit more. He had to leave, so I was left alone and started to get paranoid. Then some drunk friends came over. Drunk friends plus a bad acid trip equals a bad combination. They left, and eventually I came down. Subsequently, I stopped doing acid and greatly reduced pot and hash use after that. They were no longer the same for me.

Enter cocaine in 1977. I was seventeen and would begin drinking legally in bars the following year. Sometime in the late seventies to early eighties, coke became all the rage. It was a great complement to alcohol, which as a depressant might knock you out, but cocaine would keep you up. So you could do terrible things and not remember them the next day. And I hope to never again experience the despair I felt when coming down from an alcohol and coke bender. I often questioned whether I even wanted to live at all.

By 1977 I was good enough to start playing gigs with different bands to make money. One of the perks of being a musician was free drinks when you played! Another perk? People liked to turn the band on to whatever drugs they had. In the eighties, that usually meant cocaine. My addictions were now in full swing.

Drug and alcohol addictions feed the lowest part of yourself. The more you use the worse you feel, not just because of the physical toll it takes, but more so the mental one. And I was at a substantial level of drug and alcohol addiction. You learn to hate yourself. You know all the reasons why you're a bad person and you start to believe nothing will ever work out for you. You hurt everyone you love. You lose the things you care about the most. You lie. You cheat. And, eventually, you forget what love feels like. You start questioning if life is worth living—because at that point, when you're at your lowest, it doesn't seem like it is.

Friday the thirteenth of May 1988 began a series of events that would change my life from that point forward. I will try to describe it here as best as I can. I had been living with a woman for about three years. Prior to that, I had never been faithful to any woman I had a relationship with, including her. Infidelity was a large part of the self-loathing I carried. Up to that point, I had lost every woman I ever cared about in my life because of it.

The previous night, Thursday the 12th, our band played a club in Oshkosh, where I met another girl and went to her place after the show. We fooled around, and she told me that Sunday was her college graduation party and I should come. My live-in girlfriend would be out of town that day, so the plan was set for me to attend.

On the night of Friday the 13th, we performed a show in Fond du Lac, WI, about fifteen minutes away from Oshkosh. Our band members were known as partiers, and we all drank so much that we often traveled together in the band's truck, trying to keep one of us sober enough to drive. Unfortunately, that night I had my own car, which I had just picked up from having had some work done.

I remember that car as a three-hundred-dollar black Duster, hand painted black by the previous owner, who had also hand painted the hubcaps red. The car leaned to one side. The gas tank leaked, so you couldn't fill it up all the way. No speedometer. There was a hole by the PRNDL stick, from where you could see the road underneath the car. The driver's side door didn't work either, so you had to get in through the passenger's side and slide over.

At the end of the night, the bar manager said, "Play four more songs, and I'll give you an extra $20 and a bottle of Jagermeister, which I'll leave on the bar for you guys to drink while you load out." So, of course, we did. I mainly drank shots while the other guys loaded out.

Truck loaded. Time to drive home. There are a lot of bars on Main Street in Fond du Lac, and many cops patrol the area during bar time. I knew this. I also knew I was in no shape to drive. So, I thought, "I'll just sleep in my car until morning and then drive home." That may have been a good idea, except for the vial of white cross (speed) I had taken earlier. I may have used cocaine as well. I couldn't sleep. I decided just to try and take it easy and make it home.

I started driving down Main Street. My car had no speedometer, but I'm trying to "take it easy." At the end of Main Street, I needed to turn left to head back to Oshkosh. If I went straight, I would have entered a park. There's a statue by the park entrance. In a mental fog, I missed the turn, and as I'm trying to figure out what happened—BAM! I hit the curb by the statue going full bore. My car somehow makes it over to the side of the road, and—WHIRRR... Cherries... Cop right behind me. He was actually getting ready to pull me over for speeding because, apparently, I was going 40 in a 25 MPH zone—while trying to take it easy. I get out of the car (by the passenger's side door), walk over and say, "Just take me in. I'm way over the drunk driving limit." So they did. At the police station, I had to take the breathalyzer test. I was .29—almost three times the limit. They found the white cross vial on me, but I had taken it all. Just dumb luck there. No drug charge. But I did get an overnight stay in jail. And my car was totaled.

The next day my live-in girlfriend came to get me out of jail and was less than thrilled to see me. That night the band was scheduled to play in Montello, so the guys picked me up for the gig later in the day. By the time I woke up on Sunday my girlfriend was gone, and I was set to go to the party of the girl I had met on Thursday. Looking back now, it's hard to believe I lived like this, but that was my reality.

It was her college graduation party, a lot of people were there, so my host was busy. I started talking to another girl whom I had seen previously at our shows. We got along great. I suggested we head to a local bar together, and I left the party with this new girl, Kelly. I thank God every day for putting Kelly at that party that day.

I did not go home that night. I did not go home Monday night, either. I stayed at Kelly's. After two days I decided I loved her, and we would be moving in together. I went home on Tuesday to face the woman I had been with for three years to tell her I was leaving and that I was going to live with Kelly. There are better ways to end relationships. It tore her heart out. Worst breakup ever. I packed a bag and moved in with Kelly.

But I still had this OWI to deal with. It was my second offense. My first one was in 1979 when I was busted for violating the "no left turn on red" law. My blood-alcohol level was .29 that time too. The police didn't keep me overnight in 1979. They did make me take a class to get my license back. We called it "dumb-dumb school." That first offense was already off my record, but I still lost my license and had to undergo an assessment after this 1988 arrest.

The assessment was to determine the next course of action for me to get my license back. Most people back then got sent to "dumb-dumb school." The purpose of the assessment was to try and assess attendees' dependence on alcohol. I told Kelly the assessment was nothing, I'll just lie my way through, they'll put me in dumb-dumb school, and I'd get my license back. Her response? "Well, if you have to lie your way through, maybe you do have a problem with alcohol." Uh, wow. Wait… What? Nobody talked to me like that! It was blatantly obvious I did have a problem with alcohol, but I had built up some serious walls that prevented anyone from actually suggesting this idea to me directly. Kelly was the one person I had enough respect for who could say this to me and actually make me think about it instead of responding in anger.

I went to the assessment and decided to be a little more "honest" about my drinking than I had originally planned. Even though the first OWI was off my record, the assessor knew about it. And I was kinda/sorta honest about my drinking. Not totally honest because I wasn't quite there yet. At the end of the session, the assessor looked at everything and decided what the plan of action would be. Although I was ready to go back to dumb-dumb school, he said, "Well, based on what I see here and you already having attended the driver's ed program back in 1979, I recommend you instead go to the "personal inventory program" (PIP) for further evaluation on whether or not you have a problem with alcohol abuse."

Aw, heck. I didn't know there was something else they could put you in! Why was I honest? Damn it, Kelly!

The PIP program was basically ten court-ordered alcoholics in a room denying their alcoholism. You were not supposed to drink or use drugs during the entire program, but we all did. At that point, I was ready to start thinking that maybe I did have a problem, though. Before I went through PIP, I had always viewed AA as a "God" program. I thought the program replaced your addiction to alcohol with an addiction to God. At the time I considered myself an agnostic. It was my way of not taking AA's twelve steps too seriously.

My PIP counselor Mike was fantastic. Just the right person at just the right time for me. I stayed after almost every session to further discuss things with him. He got me to look at the chapter to the agnostic in the AA big book. I was starting to think I might be beginning to middle stages of alcohol abuse. At the program's end, you had to have a one-on-one with your counselor, and he determined the next course of action, if any. He set the date for our meeting and asked me to bring Kelly along.

On the day of the meeting, Mike pulled out a highlighter and a Jellinek Chart, which details the stages of addiction and recovery. He then said, "What we're going to do, Dave, is go through the Jellinek Chart and highlight everything that applies to you to see where you are. Kelly is here to make sure you don't lie to me."

The chart's sections denoted the beginning, middle and late stages of alcoholism. I was ready at the time to consider I that I may have been in the beginning or middle stages. "Blackouts, aggressive behavior, resolutions fail…" Highlight. Highlight. Highlight. Kelly ratted me out on a couple. By the end, the entire chart was highlighted. On the bottom of the page, in bold letters, it read "CHRONIC ALCOHOLIC." Mike said, "There it is in black and white, Dave. What are you going to do about it?"

The room got small. I have never before or since felt this sensation. It actually closed in on me. I was backed into a corner of my own making. He continued, "I recommend treatment starting next week. I'll go get your counselor, and I'll be right back." I looked at Kelly for help. She said something along the lines of "I think it'll be a good idea, Dave. Blah blah blah." She was on their side. Damn it.

This time, God brought me an angel who absolutely was the best person at the best time to help me pull myself out of my addiction. The treatment program was outpatient—four nights a week, three hours per night, for two to three months, then a follow up periodically, and AA on your own after that. I don't know where I'd be today without Dede, my counselor, had I not met her that day. To this day, I love her with all my heart. She'll be the first to say I was the one who did all the work, but this student needed a teacher. I can't think of anyone better to have guided me at that time.

Treatment started on the day after Halloween on Tuesday, November 1, 1988. I had come up with some ideas about how I was going to handle this. I was now ready to admit my alcoholism, so my idea was I would drink near beer and continue using every other drug I enjoyed—speed, downers, cocaine, etc... That was the plan.

On day one, Dede stated, "We don't do near beer; it keeps the habit too close to home. We don't use any other mood-altering substances while we're here, either." Shot my plan all to hell on that first day she did. And for whatever reason, on that day, I decided I was never going to use alcohol or drugs again. And I haven't. The cork went back in the bottle for good.

The first phase of quitting any addiction is to stop doing whatever it is you're addicted to. That's actually the easy part. Sustaining your recovery has to do with changing the mindset that got you there in the first place.

All the dark, negative thoughts you've had and all the things you've done while addicted are still in your psyche. They don't go away because you quit drugs and alcohol. You need to find ways to change your attitude about who you are and what you're capable of.

You don't need to be an addict, though, to realize the power of changing your life in an instant. There are so many things to beat ourselves up over. It's like our minds track everything negative we've ever done and hold onto it tightly to use against us in the future. When we think of something new we'd like to try, our minds shoot back five reasons why that's a dumb idea and uses past experiences to state the case. It happens to us all.

I don't know where you are on the angel-devil continuum, but I do know this: if you are unhappy with something, then you can change your life in an instant. You can decide to move in another direction. You can decide to look at your situation in a different way.

What follows are thoughts on many topics that I've struggled with on my path to staying sober, finding God, and learning how to love again in the past twenty-nine plus years of sobriety. I hope that in some small way the insights I've gained can help you as well.

I took my life as low as I could go. I was in jail. I had no car. I didn't love myself. I wasn't even sure I wanted to live. And I dug out of it all. We can all change our lives the instant we decide we're going to live another way. Don't be surprised if you have to hit a bottom first, though. Your lowest lows in life will set you up for your highest highs.

CHAPTER 2

fast mind, slow mind

04/11/2018

HAVE YOU EVER EXAMINED THE CONCEPT OF "SELF"? Of who you are, and why you're here? Of all the combinations of all the people in all of time, how is it that you came to be? And what brings you to this book, at this moment, to read the words within it?

You are a miracle. We all are.

Your mom and dad met, got pregnant, and had you. Not all that complicated, right? But what are the odds of you being you?

First, all your ancestors had to establish a very long lineage of baby after baby, creating a specific and unique gene pool, which created your mom and dad. Then your mom and dad—out of all the people on Earth—had to meet, mate, and get pregnant. One specific sperm had to fertilize one specific egg to produce you. The probability of all those events happening to produce you is one in ten to the $2{,}685{,}000^{th}$ power. That's one in ten followed by two million, six hundred eighty-five thousand zeroes.

To put that in perspective:

It's the probability of approximately two and a half million people (about the size of San Diego) playing a game of dice, each with a dice that has a trillion sides. Everyone rolls their dice, and they all come up with the same number.

That's never going to happen, right? Yet here you are. You beat incredible odds just to get here. So—why you? You must be a strong and powerful being with incredible talents to beat those odds, right? Nothing can stand in your way. So, is that how you see yourself? Why not?

Who are you?

You are not your name. You are not your occupation. You are not the things that happen to you. You are not your body. You are not the objects you look at. What's left? Thoughts?

But—weren't you here before you had language? When you were a baby? Doesn't the experiencer of thoughts exist even when thoughts are not present? Thoughts can stop, and they can also get extremely noisy. Ever have one of those days when your thoughts were driving you crazy? Who is it that is aware of the thoughts, and who is it that struggles with them? You are not your thoughts; you are simply aware of them.

There is a part of you that sits back and watches. Who you are is the one who sees. You are a spiritual being who is having a human experience, and you live in the seat of consciousness. Behind it all, you are there. I call this part of us the "slow mind." It's the part of us that knows only love. When we're in sync, when we feel like we're "in the zone," or very close to God during prayer or meditation, we are getting to know that part of ourselves. And when we have "head vs. heart" discussions with ourselves, it's the part of us that is the "heart." It's where our intuition comes from. Have you ever had something laid out in front of you that looked great on paper, but you just had this "feeling" that you shouldn't do it? The seat of your soul is your connection to God, and it's where we all reside. We just don't visit that part of us enough to follow its guidance.

I have often said that, to me, conscious contact with God is the most important thing in life. And for me, in many ways, I believe that God and love are synonymous. So how do we bring more God, more love, more light into our lives? We have to get in touch with that part of us that knows love only—our slow mind.

There's another mind, of course—our "fast" mind. This is the part we can't shut off. The one that narrates life for us. The one that we're referring to when we say, "My thoughts are driving me crazy."

The fast mind has a tendency to take over. It is relentless because it's always there, it never shuts up, it bounces from subject to subject, and it knows all the reasons why we can't do or say or be the things our heart longs for… and it's relentless. Does it shut off when we sleep? Not really. We simply enter into a different level of consciousness.

How would you feel if someone outside your own head started talking to you the way your inner voice does? They never shut up, bouncing from place to place, always critical, and having conversations with themselves. Do you ever do that? Have a conversation with yourself? Take both sides of an argument? "I think maybe we should replace the carpeting in this room, the current stuff is looking a little raggedy…yeah, but that's expensive, and we just bought a new car, and the old carpet isn't really that bad…true, but the carpet I'd like to buy is on sale, and…" Well, you get the picture. We have such conversations with ourselves all the time. So how many people are actually in there? I mean, really?

What if our thoughts were someone outside our body, sitting on the couch with us having this carpet conversation by themselves? We'd slide over, right? Maybe we'd find a way to get the heck out of there? This person is a lunatic! Yet every day we don't search for the love that exists in the seat of our consciousness—every day we don't actively seek to enhance our relationship with God—we're giving that lunatic more control over our lives.

The fast mind loves routine. The fast mind is quick to anger. The fast mind loves to control all situations. The fast mind is easily rattled.

Ever have a day in which things are going along fine then something happens? The computer system goes down, you get a call that your kid had an accident, someone cancels a big contract you were planning to close, and it affects the rest of the day after that? You can't let it go. It "sticks in your craw." Man, that's frustrating. We all have a choice in how we view such events. And if we don't actually work on how we process what happens to us in life, then often anger becomes our default setting.

How much time do we have on Earth? Maybe eighty years? Ninety? Tomorrow is guaranteed to no one. Why spend it being angry about something we can't control? That's easy to say—but hard to do.

By the way, who exactly is upset? Your computer goes down at work—instant anger and frustration as you lose a project you've been working on for the past two hours. Is it you that's upset? Or is it the lunatic on the couch next to you who's upset? We have a tendency to let that crazy person drive our thoughts and emotions. The fast mind can be laser-focused, driven and obsessive. It wants what it wants when it wants it, and if it doesn't go that way, it will not be happy. There will be hell to pay. There will be upset.

In the short time we have on this planet, who would you choose to spend more time with—the lunatic on your couch or the part of you that knows only love? Which then brings me to the question "Why don't we spend more time in prayer and meditation?" An old Zen saying states "Everyone should spend twenty minutes a day meditating, unless you're busy. In that case, take an hour."

The more we identify with the stream of thoughts we can't turn off, the further away we get from our hearts. Get in touch with your heart again. The more you know the seat of your consciousness—that part of you that can never die—the more you will see the effect it will have on your life. Because when you change the way you look at things, the things you look at change.

Wouldn't we all like, in some way, to lead a life of significance? To feel like we've made a difference? To know we left something behind for future generations? To realize we made the world a better place? But will we get there if we let our fast minds control us?

How many of us, if given the opportunity, would accept the chance to live the life of our dreams if it meant uprooting everything we have in place? I mean really do it. It's always easier to stay with what you know.

If given the chance to do something in which our hearts are saying, "Go for it! Go for it!" but it's not a sure thing—you'd have to move, quit your job, take a huge risk—most people would play it safe, and end up living their lives wondering, "What if we had actually done that?"

What if the world's greatest songwriters, authors, scientists and business-men had just settled for making a living because it was the norm? What if... Einstein worked on an assembly line—The Beatles got hotel jobs—Hemmingway became a blacksmith—and none of them followed their hearts? How sad for the rest of us. God had this amazing plan for them, but they didn't take it.

Are you taking yours?

One in ten to the $2,865000^{th}$ power chance that you're here at all, and you made it.

You have an undetermined amount of time, but we know that life is a sexually transmitted terminal disease—so it will end. And when it does, will you die with your dreams still in you?

Get in touch with that part of you that knows only love. When your fast mind starts racing, remember—this is not you. This is the lunatic on your couch. Do not give him the keys to your asylum. Let your asylum be ruled by love and surrender to the opportunities you're given as God's plan for you might just be more than you can currently imagine.

CHAPTER 3

mind-body connection

04/12/2018

I HAVE THIS THING I CALL "THE BUMP." The bump is the part of the body, just above the beltline on a pair of pants, where fat builds up—on me anyway. I hate the bump. Well, hate is a strong word. But the bump has been with me for many years. At the very least, I have a strong dislike for it. I'd love to get rid of it. So why don't I? Getting rid of the bump is a goal I could totally set and attain. This is an issue that's bothered me for years, but I still haven't set that goal. I do watch it, though, and there are limits I won't let myself go beyond. But, for the most part, I just live with it as-is because even though I'm not nuts about it, the work needed to get rid of it seems worse to me than just living with it the way it is. I'm comfortable with my body, but I'm almost never satisfied.

When I look at photos taken years ago, I often think, "Man, I looked great back then!" (Except maybe for the clothes). But if I went back to the day the photo was taken and peeked inside my head, I'd see I wasn't all that happy. I thought I was fat, or my hair looked dumb, or I was self-conscious about something else. Looking back now, I think, "Thin, good looking, and I had hair! Look at that hair!" But back then I thought, "Fat, dumb looking, and I never know what to do with my hair. I look like crap." I'm sure I am not the only person who does this to himself. I truly doubt that I am.

I've had struggles with weight my entire adult life. I stand at 5'9" and have weighed as much as 195 lbs. and as low as 155. When I hit 195, I was thoroughly disgusted with myself. I was really trying to lose weight, running two-plus miles every day, seven days a week. Yet I remained at 195 and was scared I would actually go over 200 if something didn't change. And I'm a vegetarian! I thought I had my nutrition under control. Most of what I ate was healthy. But I couldn't drop any weight.

Around that time, Nutrisystem came out with a vegetarian plan, so I thought, "What the hell. I'll take a shot." I signed up for three months. They sent me packaged food and I supplemented as needed around their meal plans with food from the grocery store. On the vegetarian plan, I ate five times a day: breakfast, lunch, afternoon snack, dinner, and an evening snack. And I had to be really mindful of portions.

Ah…portions. Before Nutrisystem, I foolishly thought that because I was eating healthy I could eat as much food as I wanted, at anytime that I wanted, without consequence! In the three months I was on the plan, I lost thirty pounds, dropping from 195 to 165. I was still running every day, and pounds were flying off. It was incredible. I eventually dropped down to 155, a total weight loss of forty pounds.

I felt great at 155 and had a huge sense of accomplishment as well. BUT—I still had the bump. So, I wasn't totally satisfied. On the day I hit 155, my thoughts were more revolved around "another ten pounds or so to go" than they were about how good I felt. The mind is never satisfied when you hit an external goal; it just sets a new target.

Our bodies, though, can influence our thought stream. While we're on Earth, the essence of who we are is contained within our bodies.

Consider this: When you buy something that is very fragile while on a trip, and it needs to be shipped home or carefully stored in your luggage, you take extra measures to make sure it won't get damaged, right? You wrap tissue all around it, place it into a special box, bubble wrap the box, and set it in the middle of your suitcase with plenty of soft clothes around it just to ensure this precious item is cared for and protected.

How are you treating the container that holds your soul? So often we eat too much, move too little, and bury ourselves in a rut that cements us in place until we hit a bottom or get a wake-up call.

It is very difficult to love ourselves when we hate ourselves. Two of the most common ways we drag ourselves down is by being critical of our appearance and not taking our physical well-being seriously enough.

When you have a cold or the flu, would you feel up to going for a run? Going dancing? Having a party? Absolutely not because you feel like crap. You're miserable. You just want to stay in bed and get better. Your body influences your thoughts. If you don't feel good physically, if you have nothing but bad things to say about yourself when you look in a mirror, then these thoughts will affect everything else in your life. And it's very hard to pull yourself out of it.

Our minds are notorious for grabbing hold of every negative thought, feeling, and emotion that we've ever experienced, only to use it against us at a later date. So when you start thinking, "I gotta do something about my weight," you instantly hear twelve reasons from your past history of why you won't do it. This negative reaction happens from the very second you have that thought. "Oh boy, here we go again. Which diet are you going to try this time? Yeah, sure. I give it a day, and you'll give up like you always do." Sound familiar? It's your fast mind, the lunatic on your couch.

Your soul is in there too, though. No one has a fat, ugly soul. If given a chance, you can change your thoughts about who you are and what you are capable of doing by getting in touch with this part of you that is time-less and ageless. We can change our bodies physically only by first chang-ing our thoughts and then acting from a place that holds no fear—our "slow" minds. If you desire to change physically, then the only way you do it is by changing your thoughts, beliefs and actions. And it can and will be done the instant you make the decision to commit to it despite what the fast mind says.

Your body can influence your thoughts. Can your thoughts influence your body?

Physically, it's easy to see that when you eat like crap, you're going to look and feel like crap. If you don't get enough rest and run your body down, you'll get sick. You can look back and say, "Man, I ate like crap. I didn't get enough sleep, and I drank too much. And now I feel awful."

But what are you feeding your mind? What happens when you have poor mental nutrition?

I fed my mind absolute garbage for fifteen years when I was on drugs and alcohol. I knew every reason on Earth why I was a worthless human being. And that made me seriously question whether life itself was worth living. How did I pull out of it? On one day, in one instant, I made a decision not to live like that anymore. I began living with a new mindset. Everything that followed came from this new paradigm. Yes, it was the day I quit using, but the negative baggage I was holding onto from those fifteen years was substantial. I'm not sure you ever totally clean the slate of your mind from the baggage we all like to hold.

I did start reading self-help books and journaling daily. I got into books like *Think and Grow Rich* by Napoleon Hill. I've read it at least six times by now. It's a classic book. I started thinking about how my mind works, looking at more spiritual material, figuring out what and who God was for me, meditating, and getting in touch with my slow mind. It's a life-long journey.

I titled this book *Feed Your Angel* because of that time in my life. I was pulling out from the darkest lows I had ever had—from not wanting to live—to now being grateful every day for every blessing I have. And there are many. It was a long road. The devil was very strong—my fast mind had an arsenal of negative thoughts, behaviors and emotions to throw at me. And it did so vehemently. I could barely find an angel in there. You can push your soul down so far that you can hardly feel it anymore. That's where I was. And every day since then, I started to "Feed My Angel" through motivational readings, meditation and writing.

Writing can be a great help. When writing, try to get it all out. Write everything out that you don't ever want to think about. If you don't, those negative thoughts will clog you up. I'm talking about the thoughts that are so painful that you can't think about them, you don't want to think about them, you don't want to write them... Write them down. Get it out. Burn your writing when you're done. Or shred it—it doesn't matter. Love will never get through a blocked heart. Clear a pathway through all that negative clutter.

The mind-body continuum is different from the angel-devil continuum in one respect: in angel-devil the ultimate goal is to eliminate the devil entirely—to live from our slow minds only. Very few people will ever get there.

When it comes to how the mind-body continuum works, it's about finding balance. It's like a teeter-totter at rest. If negative energies and habits weigh one side down, then the other side is equally affected.

Where will you be if you keep doing what you're doing mentally and physically for the next five years? Ten years? Do you like what you see when you look in the mirror? Do you like what you hear when you talk to yourself? Are you doing things every day that make your heart stir?

We all brought ourselves to this point in our lives. What will we do next?

The choice is yours...

CHAPTER 4

the power of will (somedays never come)

04/12/2018

WE ALL HAVE THINGS THAT WE PUT OFF FOR "SOMEDAY." "Someday I'll…" write a book… get a new job… start my own business… learn how to play the piano… Each of us has our own list of things that we'll get to "someday." But like the old Creedence Clearwater Revival song states, "someday never comes." The only time we have any control over is right now, right this second. Now… and it's gone. Yesterday is a memory, and tomorrow is promised to no one. "Someday" is today—right now, right this second.

We can turn our "somedays" into reality with the power of will. For every someday you have—reframe it in a sentence that starts with "I will." For example, "Someday" I'll write a book becomes "I will write a book." Then specify a timeframe like "by the end of this year." Now you've removed a "someday" from the shelf and have replaced it with a goal. With this change in reframing, you'll very quickly find out which of your "somedays" are pipe dreams and which are the ones you're serious about. Once you have an "I will" statement in place, ask yourself, "How does that feel?" If it excites you, start working on it. If it doesn't clear it off the "someday" shelf—it was just a pipe dream.

"I will write *Feed Your Angel* by April 2018" was one of mine. I had this "someday" idea for years before I decided to make it a reality. Once I made it a goal, I was excited to get to it—a little scared, too. Often it's that bit of fear that keeps us from exploring the things we've set aside for "someday." What if it doesn't work out? What if no words come? What if it's no good? Well, at least you'll know. You'll have done it. You won't be wondering, "What would have happened if I had actually done this or that?" Turn your "somedays" into reality with the power of will.

CHAPTER 5

the emotional dump

04/13/2018

AS A SPECIES, WE SEEM FAIRLY ADEPT AT HOLDING ONTO THINGS. Collecting stuff. Wanting more. Adding it to the pile. How many of us have gone through cleaning out the property of an older relative when he or she downsizes or passes away? Lots of stuff. May mom had bags full of bags. For years, things were moved from property to property, never getting used. A lot of it was moldy or decrepit and worthless by the time we found it.

Once in a while our own stuff gets so unruly that we decide we need to get rid of a few things. We hold a rummage sale, donate what we can, or sell stuff on eBay, divesting the things we've held onto that no longer serve us. The worst of the stuff we take to the dump and toss. Nobody would want that stuff. Even we wonder why we kept it for so long.

I hate throwing out stuff. I'll keep almost anything: candy bar wrappers and chewed gum, included. Okay, not quite that bad, but it's pretty bad. I have T-shirts older than my step kids who are in their mid-thirties. Why? Different reasons I guess. Some stuff has some sort of emotional attachment like a concert I went to—when I was a size medium, so I haven't worn it in twenty years—a band I was in, or a club I played at. I have tons of old clothes: pants, shirts, jackets… I have a truly tough time parting with anything. And we also have those "boxes of things" that we look at only when we move, too. "What's in here again? Oh, yeah, Hardy Boy books!" Packed, sealed, moved, but never to be opened again.

I don't think everyone hoards, but we all have different levels of attachment to things. We all have stuff we like to hold onto, but most of us hang onto a t least a few things we have little or no use for. Which brings me back to asking why? Why would we ever think we need a bag full of bags we collected ten years ago and have never used, but that we moved with us to three different addresses? It must be the thought that the second we give something away, we'll need it! Aw shucks, I could really use that bag full of bags right now. And, of course, we've all pretty much had that happen. We got rid of something, then later needed it and wished we had kept it. So inside, our fast minds latch onto that and create this "lack" mentality that says, "Don't give anything away!" So we don't. And if we make an exception, we do it begrudgingly. The fast mind loves to hold onto things—physically and mentally.

All over the world our attics and basements are full of things we don't want, never use and have no purpose for mainly because the voice inside our head tells us we need to keep it. Can't throw anything away.

But what do we hold in the attics and basements of our minds? Isn't it the same part of us that keeps useless physical items that's also in charge of our mental inventory? Are our minds all of a sudden better housekeepers when in charge of our thoughts, feelings and emotions? No! We've got a mess in there, too! There's junk stored everywhere—everything bad that's ever happened, everyone who ever wronged us, every embarrassing moment of our life is stored in there. Why? Do you really want to relive that? Because that's what it's in there for—to scare us into not doing anything outside our comfort zones.

Let's say you have an idea to open your own bakery; baking is your passion. You bake for family and friends, and they all rave about it. They even say you should open a bakery. But you've had a government job for more than ten years. It pays well, offers a pension, provides a steady paycheck… and if and when you start to seriously consider doing anything different, wham! Let's head up to the attic in our mind and see what we have in our boxes... Oh! Remember when you wanted to start a lemonade stand when you were six, and nobody bought any lemonade except your mom? You couldn't even sell lemonade, but now you want to give up a job you've held for ten years—salary, pension and benefits—to start a bakery? Ha! Fat chance.

Everything bad that's ever happened to us is stored in boxes in the attics and basements of our minds. Just like our actual junk, it gets tucked away and we forget about it.

If we hoard too much of our material stuff, it makes it hard to get around our homes. Maybe you create paths between the junk, but what if an entire room of your house was filled with junk you'll never use? So full that if you tried to get into that room, you couldn't—it's jam packed with boxes. Want to open the window on the other side of the room? No way. Can't do it. You're blocked.

Most of us have similar junk rooms in our minds that are completely blocked. If you create enough of them, then the entire house becomes junk—with you stuck in the middle. There's no way out.

We periodically go through and clean up our material junk, so why don't we do it with the mental baggage? Like the stuff we carry from house to house, once it's in, we forget about it. Yet it continues to build up, creating blockages.

All the negative mental baggage we carry blocks us from knowing and expressing who we truly are. It's like we're sitting in the middle of a house filled with junk—and God is outside. How will we ever get to know Him when we're so blocked we can't even get to a window or a door to let Him in?

Hopefully, your situation is not quite this dire, but we all have emotional baggage we carry with us. We don't want to go there. We don't want to think about it. Does hiding it really do us any good?

Let's say we did something absolutely horrible. We stole something very valuable from our best friend. A rare and valuable piece of jewelry. You absolutely loved it and had to have it, so you stole it. You feel terrible about it—embarrassed, sad. It's an awful thing to think about, and you can't share the story with anyone. And you can't even sell the jewelry because if it went on the market, you'd get caught. So you hide it amongst the junk boxes with the old VHS tapes at your house. It's there, though. You know it's there. After some time, you forget about it a little, but every once in a while, you think about it and it bothers you, so you push the feelings out of your mind.

One day a family member comes over and asks, "Hey, do you still have those old VHS tapes? My kid needs a few for an art project." and you freak out. Then you start worrying the stolen jewelry could be found there, and maybe you need a better hiding spot, and perhaps your friend has known all along you took it, and... that piece of jewelry controls you for the rest of your life because you weren't able to take it out and deal with it. That's what happens when we box up the negative, painful memories of our past, and never look at them. They build up. Our fast minds control us. They'd rather we didn't get in touch with God because they'd lose control. So they box everything up and create an obstacle course of baggage to wade through to get there.

Every chance you get, take your baggage to the emotional dump. Let it go like you would an old couch. Smash it and walk away. One way to get started is to write it all out as I discussed in chapter three on the mind-body connection. Sit down and write out everything you hold as resentment—Billy Peterson socked you in the arm in second grade, and you're still mad. Write it down. It doesn't have to be reasonable or make any sense. In fact, much of it shouldn't make any sense at all. Get it out. Get it out. Get it out!

The emotional baggage we hold onto not only stops us from going within ourselves to know our slow minds, but it also affects our ability to let love and joy flow from us.

Wayne Dyer once said, "When you squeeze an orange, you get orange juice. What do people get when they squeeze you?" Anger? Someone goes digging around the junk boxes of your mind and they rip one open that you didn't ever want to look at. What's your response? Love? It should be. My guess, though, is that's not the case.

Getting rid of everything we've been holding for years is just part of the battle. Don't clean it out just to fill it with more junk—more anger and more resentments. How do we learn not to take everything so personally? By getting in touch with and living our lives from the place that knows love only—our slow minds—God, the seat of our consciousness. By noticing when the lunatic on our couch starts getting upset and stepping back into God rather than going there. We're so accustomed to letting the voice that narrates our lives run everything that we've forgotten who we are is not that voice. Who we truly are is behind that voice, watching.

How do you know when your mind is arguing with itself? Aren't you one of the people arguing? Or, wait...no, you're both of the people arguing. If that's so, then who's watching the argument? The argument is the lunatic. The essence of who you are is the one who watches. Everything blocking the path between you and that part of you that watches—the slow mind—needs to be dealt with if you truly seek spiritual progress.

overcoming our addiction to ego

04/14/2018

WHAT SEPARATES AN OBSESSION FROM AN ADDICTION? You can be obsessed with something, but not be addicted to it. Some people would say I'm somewhat obsessed with the Green Bay Packers. I've been a fan my whole life and know almost every player on the team, including the practice squad and injured reserve. I watch every game live, including pre-season. But I wouldn't consider it an addiction. I wouldn't steal to get money to buy Packers tickets. I wouldn't use mortgage money to buy memorabilia. I wouldn't consider suicide if they lost a game. The difference is you can have fun with an obsession without it having a negative effect on your life. An addiction, on the other hand, will mess you up.

You can be obsessed with all kinds of worthwhile things. Finding God, for example, would usually be a worthwhile obsession. Working out. Accumulating collectibles—stamps, coins, beer cans, etc... Making music, skiing, mountain climbing, or running. You could be obsessed with any or all of these without being addicted. Some of them might even be worthwhile endeavors. But any obsession could also become an addiction once it starts destroying our inner peace.

Alcohol, drugs, debt, sex, food and gambling—these are the addictions we hear about most often. Problems in these areas have hurt people and broken up families throughout the world and continue to do so today. But all the things I mentioned as obsessions in the prior paragraph can become addictions as well. The hole in your heart can never be filled with an external addiction. They will always make it worse.

Addictions also like to travel in packs. Let's say you begin by abusing alcohol and drugs. You get sucked in; you get hooked. You now need an even bigger high, so you go to the local casino and start gambling. What a rush! Drinking, using, gambling—and then you start meeting other people, and having extramarital affairs. One day you wake up with a hole in your heart that's bigger than ever. You realize that you've spent all your money (now you're also having debt issues), you didn't go home, you slept with a stranger, so—what do you do? Eat! You eat as much as possible because you gotta fill that emotional hole. You're now in a vicious, vicious cycle of despair and anxiety.

All addictions have different methods for recovery, too. Alcohol and drugs, for example, are straightforward. Step 1: Stop using alcohol and drugs! If you use, you're not recovering.

But what about an addiction to food? Stop eating? You have to eat. How can you tell if you're in recovery, then? You're addicted to food, but you have to eat. Well, you need to modify your habits because you can't stop entirely or you'll die.

The reason addictions travel in packs is this: if you have a hole so deep in your heart that you'll do anything not to face that pain, and you've convinced yourself the answer will be found anywhere else but from looking within, then you'll try whatever you can to get even a small period of time when the pain is forgotten, no matter the future cost.

This is why on day one of alcohol treatment I was told "no mood altering substances allowed because they are all equal," which trashed my plan to use every drug except alcohol once in treatment. Switching an alcohol addiction to a pot addiction doesn't do anything. Inside, you still have a huge hole to fill. A huge, empty hole where love belongs, and you have nothing. Having no love brings great sorrow.

How does the definition of addiction relate to our ego if the term means something we're so obsessed with that it messes up our lives because we keep going back to it, thinking it will fill the emptiness we feel inside when all it ever does is make it worse? Aren't we all addicted to our ego?

Who do we listen to when we want to buy that car we shouldn't buy and can't afford? The ego! We deserve it!... and the payments create more stress, and it breaks down, and there's no money to repair it because things are tight, so we start snapping at each other... remember: you deserve it!

What about when opportunity knocks? The chance of a lifetime—right there, within your grasp. Who is the voice of reason that talks you out of it? Your ego.

We're all addicted to the fast mind. The ego tells us that we need this, we need that, we can't do this, though, too risky. The ego develops ruts over time—deep, cavernous ruts that it never wants messed with. Just try to step outside a long-standing routine and listen to the fast mind object. What are you thinking?

At some point, we tend to get okay with how things are. The attic and the basement of our minds are slightly cluttered, but we can get around. Heck, we have these ruts now and as long as we never step outside to try anything new, we're totally fine in here. But are we?

Why do we get mad when someone is driving too slow in front of us? I'm as guilty as anyone here—this bothers me. Why? Well, I'd like to go faster. What difference will it make? I'd get there one to two minutes sooner. Will you be happier getting there sooner? Probably, because this guy's making me angry. What if he wasn't making you angry and you got there two minutes later. Would it matter? Uh...no. So the slow-moving car squeezed you a little, and anger came out. Why are you so angry?

Whoa.

If you're getting angry because the car in front of you is driving too slow, or the mail wasn't delivered on time, or it's raining out and you may get wet—little things—then catch yourself. Right there. Catch yourself.

Those are small squeezes, so why are you so angry? What will happen when you get truly bad news? Like a tree falls on your house, you need a twenty-thousand-dollar repair, and your insurance won't cover it. My God, your head would explode.

We aren't just obsessed with the non-stop voice inside our heads, we're addicted to it. It controls almost everything we say or do. You work a job until you're sixty-five, you retire, then you die. That's what everyone does. But, what if I…No, no…we're on this path here. Do you remember that one time you tried something outside your ruts? How did that go? Terrible, right? No, we're safe here, this is how it is…

And the more the ego controls us the more emotional baggage we store, and the angrier we get. It's how we turn into "old man high pants," yelling at kids to stay off our lawn. The emotional baggage has been repressed for so long that anger is the only thing left, and anything other than anger doesn't feel right. This is no way to live.

We need to break free from our addiction to ego. How? Well, we can't turn off the fast mind. Would be nice if we could. We can at best hope for moments of peace during meditation, but much like an eating addiction, the ego can't be turned off.

Can we change the narration?

Yes. Yes, we can. And the only way to do this is by looking within ourselves. Through it all, our God presence—our slow mind—is waiting. Waiting for us to realize that all the love we've ever needed was and already is inside us, waiting to be unleashed. Like overcoming any addiction, step one is admitting that we're powerless. The ego has a hold on our lives. Do we want to change that? If we do, then we need to change the way we look at things and start to realize that our egos are on auto-pilot. Because we can catch ourselves. We can catch ourselves when letting anger well up over small things. And when we do, each time we do, we're taking a step in the right direction.

We can spend more time getting to know our slow minds. As we do, the peace and love that emanates from that part of us will take back control of our emotions. How can we be angry if we know only love?

We can begin to remove the blocks we've allowed to remain in our mental attics and basements. Pull them out, look at them, deal with them, and then let them go. You will find deep-seated stuff way in the back that you won't want to let go of. Those are the most important blocks you'll need to contend with. That's probably not where you want to start, but pull the box out. Look at the issue. Start at least thinking about letting it go. What would that feel like? Why are all these boxes, packed years ago, still in there stopping you from knowing God and letting love be what people see when they squeeze you?

Because you're addicted to your ego. So am I. We all are.

You have an endless ocean of love within you. If each of us simply tried to get in touch with that part of ourselves on a daily basis, we could change the entire world. That will only happen if we all do our part. The only mind we control is our own. I'll do my part if you do yours...

Deal?

sadness

04/15/2018

SADNESS IS A TOUGH SUBJECT FOR ME TO DISCUSS. Every once in a while, I'll have a day where I'm sad for no reason at all. Nobody died. Nothing got broken. I didn't get turned down for a promotion. No reason at all, but totally sad. And even though I know nothing in my exterior world is creating this sadness, I'm still sad. And I can't "positive think" my way out of it. Where is this coming from?

If nothing exterior is causing it, then a deeper issue is lying underneath the surface. Do you think God ever has a "mopey" day? When we seek the presence of God within us, do we ever get there and find anything but love? No! We were made in God's image—like a glass of water being taken from the ocean, we're a cup of God—yet He is never sad, but we are. Why? Where does the sadness come from?

Even when we're happy, we're sometimes sad. Ever have that happen to you? Things are just clicking right along, everything's going great, got a vacation coming up, and down in your heart you still feel some sadness. Like an underlying current that says, "We're not totally good in here yet." It's just enough to be noticeable, but not bothersome. What do you do?

If you're like most people, you do nothing. You just blow the sadness off. Act like you never noticed it. Don't say anything about it to anyone. It's nothing. But is it?

Our life can look great on the surface while a war rages inside of us. When we follow the guidance of our egos—which can be focused and driven—we can get a lot done, make a lot of money, drive a nice car, and live in a great neighborhood. But inside we can be miserable because our lives have become monotonous from the ruts our egos have attached to.

How many times a day do you feel extreme joy? In a month? A year? For many of us, it might just be once or twice, very briefly, in a year—if at all. I'm talking about a joy that says, "I want the rest of my life to be just like this very moment in time." But we don't get to feel like that very often.

How about love? How many times a day do you feel love? Now, here's an emotion we can touch and feel every day if we wanted to. We simply need to make it a priority. Do you? Or do you run out the door, race to your job, drive back home, eat a quick dinner, watch TV and go to bed, not ever exchanging any real love at all? Maybe you "love" your job, but even a job you love won't give you many opportunities to actually feel the emotion of love.

Can you start to see now where everything can be going well, but inside you're sad? The opposite of love can be debated, but for now let's just say it's hate. I either love you, or I hate you. What emotion do you feel when you lose or lack love?... Sadness.

You have a car you absolutely love, and it gets totaled. Sadness. The pet you've had for fifteen years passes away. Sadness. Losing what you love makes you sad. But what if we lack love? You never find a soulmate, or you're in a relationship and the spark went out years ago, so you don't share real love anymore. That's sad. And that sadness will build over time. So when you noticed that maybe there was an undercurrent of sadness, but you decided it was nothing and you blew it off—several times over a period of weeks or months—maybe the real question should be: Why don't we have *more* days where we're sad and can't pull out of it?

The only way to combat sadness is to get more love into your life. What we often do when we search for love is to look outside ourselves. But once again, love is an inside job. We have all the love we need to access available right inside ourselves if we simply choose to look for it and then live from that space. It sounds so easy, but it isn't. It's a lifelong process.

There's more to it than just finding ways to add love into our lives. What other issues aren't we really looking at? We get very good at just going day in and day out with living an existence that's okay, but not truly fulfilling. We all need endeavors in our lives that we do simply because we love them so much. Are there unfulfilled dreams inside of you? Do you like to paint? Write songs? Build things? Have your favorite passions from years ago gone by the wayside because you "don't have the time" or "weren't any good at"?

Is it possible to stay sad if you spread love and joy to others? Next time you're sad, surprise someone with a gift. "Here, Sally, we were talking about this book the other day, so I got you a copy. I hope you like it!" What will Sally's reaction be? Surprise! Happiness! She'll hug you and tell you how you're the best friend ever. Now how do you feel? Better?

The more we know love and the more we spread love to others, the happier we'll be. Eventually, we can live from that place where we know only love; it just takes time. And practice. Seek love today for happier tomorrows.

time

04/15/2018

"THE TROUBLE IS, YOU THINK YOU HAVE TIME." This quote is often attributed to Buddha, and the younger we are, the more the message seems to fit. As young people, we think we have all the time in the world. We have big plans we're going to accomplish. Then… (blink)— we missed it. That's how time works. The older we get the faster it moves, too. And time is guaranteed to no one.

How shall we spend our time, then? We have so little of it, and every day it speeds up on us. What, then, is the most important thing to focus on? How about "enjoy the present moment" since that's all we really have control over? A friend I met on the internet years ago always said, "Enjoy whatever happens." What a great philosophy for life, but is it possible? I guess it depends on whether we think it is or not. As Henry Ford said, "Whether you think you can or think you can't, you're right." So as long as we believe it to be possible, then yes, it is possible. It's not what most of us are doing. But it is possible.

So, basically, God dropped us down on this interesting and amazing planet with all kinds of incredible stuff to see and do—and we decided to do the same thing every day, so that we can make enough money to be able to retire someday when we're too old to actually go and enjoy anything. Do we have other options? Of course we do. But did we consider them—seriously consider them? Probably not.

"Before enlightenment: chopping wood, carrying water. After enlightenment: chopping wood, carrying water." This Buddhist saying reminds us that what we do isn't important. What is important is how we feel about what we're doing. My previous example of working a job to earn enough money to retire but then being too old to enjoy it is pretty grim. But what if the job we worked was as much fun as a vacation? So many of us slog through days at the mill to get a week or two of pseudo-relaxation (you know you have to go back to work on Monday), then right back at it until we retire or drop dead. Spiritual growth is when you have love in your heart through it all. You don't need to wait for vacation. The machine breaks down, a client calls and yells at us—we stay calm and observe. "Wow! Look at the challenges today! My machine broke! We haven't done this in a while." We learn to enjoy whatever happens.

This doesn't mean we stay in bad situations. If we have a terrible work environment, we simply take it one day at a time—with love in our heart—until we find something else and be grateful the first job was so awful that it made us go find the next job, which we love—as is often the case when we make changes in life. We change because we bottom out, and those bottoms can be the best things that ever happen to us when we use them as inspiration for change.

It's crazy how fast time moves. We really have so little of it. Who determines whether we spend time happy or sad? Isn't that up to us? Or have you handed over your happiness to the lunatic on your couch? If that guy's in charge, then you're in trouble. And for the vast majority of us, that's the way it is.

How many times have we heard that "time flies when you're having fun"? Well, it sure does. That might be why the older you get the faster it goes. When we're older, we typically have a better handle on spiritual matters, and time moves faster the more you learn to enjoy it.

What kind of a split would you like to have between happy and everything else (sad, angry, afraid, anxious, etc.)? 50/50? Is 50% happy good enough? Is it? Where do you think your ratio actually sits right now? 50/50 might not be that far off, right?

Being anxious and worried and sad and angry eats up way too many of our very limited hours on Earth. We are not that part of us that gets upset; we are just watching that part of us as if it were sitting next to us on the couch. The more you look within, get to know God, live from a place of love, and take control away from your fast mind, then the happier you will be and the better your present moments will be. The present moment is all we can control. So why on Earth would we do anything except to enjoy whatever happens?

anticipation, anxiety, guilt, worry and shame

04/16/2018

I FIND IT DIFFICULT TO RELAX because my ego has been such a strong part of me throughout my life that it's hard to shut it off. It's seemingly always upset about something. There's a lot of anxiety and worry. If I have an event coming up, no matter what it is—let's say dinner with friends at six o'clock—that event is on my mind all day long. I'm thinking, "Well, I better get home by four, so I can change clothes. We'll have to let the dog out. The restaurant is thirty minutes away. I hope they're not busy. Why are we going on a Friday night? They're going to be busy. Maybe I should call the other couple to make sure they're on time." And on and on. This is the way my mind works when I'm just having dinner with friends! What is that? The present moments are being eaten up by thoughts about how to even just get to a dinner that's hours away. Ever hear the saying, "The anticipation is killing me"? Ever feel that? I do all the time. That's your future stealing your nows away.

What about guilt and shame? You get invited to a birthday party and ask your friends who else will be there? "Well, Bob and Sue, John from the liquor store, Ed from work… and Betty. Betty will be there."

"Betty? Yeah, I might skip it then. I don't want to see Betty. I told her I'd help at the pancake breakfast last week, and I totally forgot and left her shorthanded. I heard she's pretty mad about that. I can't face her yet." We've all avoided people, places and situations that made us uncomfortable because of something that happened in the past.

We let anxiety and worry ruin present moments by anticipating what may or may not happen in the future, and we let guilt and shame do the same thing with past events. Do we ever just enjoy the moment?

In his talks, Michael Singer uses the analogy of a first kiss. We meet someone. We start dating. It's all going well. Then there's that moment when you finally just kiss each other for the first time. For that instant, you're in the moment.

We're very seldom in the moment. Instead, we live our lives in the past and in the future without spending much time just learning how to be here now. When you're having a conversation, are you in the moment? Or are you spending more time thinking about your response than actually listening? We dance all around our present moments instead of being one with them.

I've already discussed how to start dealing with guilt and shame in previous chapters. These things are usually contained in the baggage from our past. All that embarrassing stuff you did—dig it up and let it go. The better you get at this, the less likely you are to add in new problems. Instead, you'll start to deal with it as it comes up.

For example, let's revisit the story about not going to the birthday party because Betty might be there. Rather than letting your guilt control you—not going, and probably exacerbating the situation—you realize that when Betty's name was brought up, you felt some guilt. You accept the invite, and since you don't DO guilt, you contact Betty and clear things up before you go to the party rather than trying to avoid her. No baggage.

Now, maybe Betty won't be open to clearing things up. Maybe she's really mad, tells you she hates you and never wants to see you again, and hangs up. How do you deal with that? More guilt and shame? For sure not going to the party? Maybe you hate her now, too? Or can you keep love in your heart toward your friend and not take on new baggage? Let her anger flow right through you without affecting you. That's the goal. See everything and everyone with love, no matter how unfair and alien it might feel to you. Very few of us will ever get there.

And that's just about the events that are behind us! Now we have to look at how we ruin present moments by thinking ahead to things that haven't even happened yet. That's actually even more ridiculous.

Let's look at a first date as an example. Remember how that felt? You set up the date—dinner and a movie, let's say for six o'clock. The whole day gets shot. You probably wake up with a pimple, so now you're self-conscious, "Oh, sure, a first date and I've got this humongous thing on my face." Now you're worried about that from the second you get up and look in the mirror. Then all day you think, "What am I going to wear? It's a nice restaurant, but then there's the movie, so I don't want to get grease on anything too nice, but I can't look like a slob. I already have this stupid pimple. I should have had my hair done. I hope I don't say anything offensive." Wow! It's a wonder any two people ever get together when you think about all the mental baggage we put ourselves through before we even get there.

Let's say dinner goes extremely well. You go to the movie, and you both love it. On the way back from the movie, you say something that obviously bothers your date. Whatever you said is viewed as insensitive when you were trying to be funny. You quickly apologize, but when you get to the door, you just hug and and go your separate ways. The vibe was lost after that "joke." What do you remember? Four hours of awesomeness or the five minutes of bad vibe? Those five minutes can kill you. Driving home, hitting yourself in the head for being so stupid—you've got some new emotional baggage now. Oh, and the whole day was spent worrying about a date that was mostly fantastic, even though all you can think about is the negative. The two of you might not ever go out again because of it. The only reason this doesn't sound ridiculous to you is because this is how we live.

How is it possible to have future baggage? We all have a fear of the unknown. Our minds like to keep us in our comfort zone, and new people and experiences pull us out of that zone where thoughts start to go crazy. Then the mind looks into its memory banks to give us a few select pieces of awfulness from our history. Let's say that previously talked about date is now in the past, and you never saw each other again. Next time you have a first date, your mind will remind you not to be such an idiot, so you'll be way more guarded, and that new person won't get the full experience of who you are because of the date you had two months earlier. You have pre-conceived notions of how things could and should go instead of just being in the moment.

Half the battle is catching yourself. When you feel guilt or shame, pull that baggage out and go through it. Clean up what you can. If you find things you're not willing to face yet, start an "on deck" circle and work up to them. Nothing will set you free more than working through the guilt and shame you feel from past events.

If and when you start obsessing over future events that haven't even happened yet, catch yourself. Get calm. See the event with love. Envision it going well. Do whatever you need to do right then to stop thinking about it until you're home and getting ready, or you're in the moment of the event itself. Don't let the future or the past steal your nows.

are you aware of your face?

04/17/2018

WE ALL KNOW PEOPLE WHO MAKE US FEEL GOOD simply by their presence. If they walk in unexpectedly, you immediately feel joy. It seems like they're always happy. I bet most of us can look back on our lives and name a few people we see that way. They exude joy and it's contagious.

How do people feel when you walk into a room? What does your expression tell people when they meet you? Are you full of joy? Why not? Aren't you happy? Are you aware of your face?

The truth is even happy people have good and bad days. In the course of a day, depending on what we're doing and who we're with, it can be very different.

You probably know people who view you as that person who lights up their life. I know that if I walk in unexpectedly on my grandkids, they'll go nuts. Grampa!... What a great feeling to be that person for others.

And then you probably know other people whom you feel quite differently about. They walk in and your heart sinks. "Oh, God! It's Ed. I can't stand that guy." Sometimes, you don't even know the person, and you instantly don't like him when he walks into the room. What is that?

It could be something to do with your past. Their mannerisms might remind you of someone you didn't get along with, so you project that dislike onto this new person. Or maybe it's just a person's general demeanor that says, "Stay away."

Chances are also good that we are all this person to other people in our lives as well. Sometimes, it's just a feeling you get. Something like, "Why doesn't he/she like me? What did I ever do?" Maybe it has nothing to do with you and everything to do with their past. And maybe, just maybe— it's you. Your demeanor. Your walls. Are you aware of your face?

Lately, I'm becoming aware that I can look unhappy or pensive, even in situations that are meant to be fun. I'm becoming more and more aware that the person I feel I am inside isn't always the person I show to people externally.

So am I happy if I don't look happy, even when I should be happy? I doubt it. To me this points to a deeper underlying issue. Your face is at the forefront of your relationship with life. We can tell ourselves whatever we want to about how we're feeling, but our face will tell the world what's really going on.

I have a network of people I contact when I need a "pick me up" because I know once I get off the phone or we meet for lunch, I'm going to leave feeling better than I did going in. I know I have people who look to me as one of those support people for them. But with a little bit of work, couldn't we get our percentages up?

I try to look at myself in the mirror and objectively see what I'm conveying to others a couple of times a day. Do I look happy? Am I happy? Way too often I see a tired, unhappy person looking back. That breaks my heart. I'm extremely aware of this.

I'll date myself a bit here. On the TV series *Cheers*, there was a character named Norm, who upon entering the bar, would be greeted by everyone shouting his name in unison: Norm! Then there was always a great one-liner joke that would follow. **Bartender:** What would you say to a beer, Norm? **Norm:** Going down? When Norm walked in, he changed the whole demeanor of the entire bar for the better.

I want to be Norm. And you can't fake it. Either you have love flowing freely from deep within you or you don't. Imagine having love flow so freely that everyone in the room is lifted up just by your presence, like they were all your grandchildren or the patrons of Cheers. Grampa!... Norm!...

Take a long, hard look at yourself. What do you see? Is there work to do? Your face is the window through which others see your soul. Make sure they have a clear pathway.

why is this happening to me?

04/18/2018

INSIDE OUR MINDS, WE ALL HAVE PRE-CONCEIVED NO-TIONS about how we'd like things to unfold. We'd like to wake up, have breakfast, ride to work, have no problems there, come home, eat dinner, and then have an evening activity. Great day. Just do that, every day. Is that too much to ask? Probably so because my guess is that at some point in your life, you've known the feeling of, "Why is this happening to me?" Am I right? Maybe even right now as you read this, you have an issue you're dealing with.

Imagine this scenario instead…you wake up and go to make coffee. It's a new container, and you're in a hurry. You pull the seal off, lose control and coffee grounds go flying everywhere. Damn it! Inside, what are you thinking? Not even five minutes into your day, and you're probably thinking, "Why does this always happen when I'm in a hurry?"

The rest of breakfast goes okay, but you're running a little late because of the coffee incident. You run out to the car, back the car out…but something's not right. You get out to have a look—and you have a flat tire. Oh, for God's sake! First the coffee, now the tire? So now you're aggravated and even more late, and you have to put one of those little "weenie" tires on your car and drive to work slower than usual. You get to work late, upset, and find out the boss wants to see you. Oh, brother! What now? You head in to see him. He's not happy, he wants major re-visions on work you thought you had already completed, and this gets added to your workload. After this unpleasant meeting, the rest of the day goes about as well as can be expected since, by now, you're frustrated and angry.

You have a nice leisurely drive home going forty-five miles an hour in a fifty-five mile zone on your little "weenie" tire, and you get home later than usual also because of the extra workload that was thrown at you, hoping your spouse might have dinner ready. But you find a note: "Went to dinner with my sister. You're on your own tonight." After you slap peanut butter on bread and wash it down with a bowl of cereal, you finally sit down to relax… and the cable is out!

Ever have a day that went like that? I hope maybe not quite that bad, but we've all had those days, and we're thinking, "Why is this happening to me?" But these might just be the most important days of our lives. How can we grow if we're never challenged?

First off, as always, ask yourself, "Who is upset?" Are you upset, or are you watching yourself be upset? Could all that bad stuff have happened, but you have an awesome day in spite of it? Of course, it could! It's not you who's upset; it's that person next to you on the couch who is freaking out. During the course of the day, he's been having conversations with himself about changing coffee brands, suing a tire company, getting a new job, whether or not your spouse loves you, and maybe even switching cable providers. Each little aggravation had its own little subset of the day in which your mind used its time to roll through a bunch of different scenarios about how you were going to get even. None of it was your fault. Stupid coffee cans should be easier to open. Tires shouldn't just go flat; that tire was obviously defective. And those reports were fine when you handed them in; you can't help it if the boss changed all the metrics. Your spouse… if you had to leave them hanging, you would have left a decent supper… they're so inconsiderate. And that cable company is going to pay for your lost time, or you're switching to satellite!

So, there you sit. Grumpy, no TV, tired, full of junk food, "weenie" tire still on your car, and maybe you haven't even picked up the coffee grounds yet. Ah, let your spouse do it. They left you hanging on dinner. And now, you're already set up to have a bad day tomorrow because of it. And your spouse better not come home all happy and giggly from dinner, either. That's the last thing you want to see.

Or…

We can take notice of when our inner peace is being threatened. We can realize that as much as we try to control everything in our lives, the truth is—we have no control. And we will be challenged. When the coffee goes everywhere, and you feel yourself get anxious and angry—whoa, slow down. This is not you. You're just watching the event unfold. Will you let the lunatic take over, or will you calm him down and realize that today is "spilled coffee day," so you're okay with that? You can be okay with that if you step back and take control rather than giving it over to the fast mind, which all too often is our default setting.

You head out, back the car up—flat tire, ha! Perfect. It's "spilled coffee, flat tire" day now. Wait until they hear about this at work. Wow! A "weenie" tire! Those things are hilarious. The car will sit at a funny angle, so you'll have to drive slowly. Yes, the fast mind will need to be calmed down. The events themselves are not aggravating, though. It's how you process the events that will determine whether you will be upset or not.

The day you realize that being upset is a choice and you don't just have to accept your default setting is the day you start moving in the direction of a much happier and fulfilling life.

It starts by catching yourself. When something hits your psyche in a way you can feel your feelings and emotions start to well up—stop! Ah, here it is—a learning opportunity. Can you stay calm? You will be challenged. How will you react?

The worst days of your life are the best days of your life. They help you grow. If you don't learn the lesson, the same issues will continue to show up until you do.

Catch yourself…

Calm yourself…

Grow.

god doesn't need language

04/18/2018 & 04/20/2018

COULD YOU FIND GOD WITHOUT USING LANGUAGE? Is that even possible for you? No books, no dogma, no words, no mantra, no step-by-step guide, no prayer—could you interact with God without using language?

To me, it's the only way we can interact with God. We go within. Words are human.

You might think you need a book that explains everything that needs to be done, and exactly how to do it. You might even be certain within yourself this is the only proper way to find God, as well. If that's true, then how did people find God before the book was written?

Could a book ever be written today that would be the correct way to find God in your life? Of course, it could. Could any of the great religious books in history help you find God? Of course, they could. But do you have to figure out which way is the best way and follow only that path or you will go to hell? Now, why would God make finding Him a multiple-choice question?

Billions of people live on this planet. No two of us are alike. There are approximately forty-two hundred different religions in the world. Do you seriously think the path that helped you find God is the only way for anyone else to find God? Are all four thousand one hundred ninety-nine other religions wrong? Almost everyone goes to hell? I can't see it.

It's like finding a huge metropolitan area that has forty-two hundred roads leading into the city. You take one of them, and it gets you there, so you think everyone else has to go the way you went, or they can't get to the city. The reality is many other roads lead to the same place. In fact, there are four thousand one hundred ninety-nine of them!

Does it then truly matter what you call the city? For example, let's use the city of Detroit to illustrate. Some people call it Motown, others Motor City. Does the city change depending on what you call it? No! Neither does God. Call Him Jesus, Allah, Buddha, Yahweh—it doesn't matter. One God, many names. No language necessary.

What is necessary is that we take as much time as possible to make conscious contact with God in our lives. How can we live from the place within our heart that knows only love if we don't actively work on that relationship?

Once you have that relationship, once you know that love, it's only natural to want to share it. You also want others to feel it. And no matter which way got you there, whatever path was put in front of you, it was just what you needed. It will also be a path that many others will take as well. But there are many paths. Let's not get so caught up in the way we find God that we forget that God is love.

If you believe, as I do, that it's possible to find God without language, then how could it possibly be true that once language is introduced and forty-two hundred religions are created that only one of them is the pathway to God?

One God, many pathways.

Look within.

Language not needed.

life

04/20/2018

YOU SET A COURSE. YOU MAKE A PLAN. AND YOU ADJUST AS YOU GO. Very seldom does everything go off without a hitch. There's a reason we're all too familiar with the saying, "Nothing ever goes as planned."

As I write this chapter, I'm on the twelfth day of the nineteen days I gave myself to finish an entire book. It's becoming quite obvious to me that it won't be as large a book as I expected it was going to be. My original idea was fifteen chapters, each taking twenty minutes to read through. This is chapter thirteen, and none of the prior chapters will take very long to read at all. I have seven days left after today. I will have more chapters in this book than I had expected, though. And that's life, right?

Even though nothing ever goes as planned, we still plan. When we're kids, people will ask, "What do you want to be when you grow up?" It's like they expect you to already have a plan. When I was very young, I made up my mind that I wanted to be a certified public accountant. I had no idea what that was, but we had accountants in my family, and I liked the way it sounded, so that became my answer. It wasn't what most adults expected to hear either. I went as far as taking an accounting class in college—and that was the end of my accounting career. Because, to me, that was not "fun with numbers." We make plans, and then we adjust.

Over time, it can become harder to make adjustments. Our lives find grooves, and adjusting out of them can be very unsettling. The older we get, the more people it can affect as well. Let's say you've worked at a factory for twenty years and made the decision you can't take it anymore, and now is the time to follow your dream and open a pizza place. You've been thinking about it, saving up, the job has been getting worse at the factory, and the timing seems perfect. You go home and tell your wife, "Honey, on Monday I'm giving my notice, and we're going to open that pizza place this year like I've always wanted to do." She looks down, dead silent. You say, "What? What's wrong? We've talked about this for years" She starts her reply with, "Yes, but…" *Oh, boy* you think. *Nothing good can come after a yes, but…* "Yes, but,"she continues, "I didn't think you would want to do it so soon. The kids have college coming up, and we have house and car payments. What will we do for health insurance? I'm really not comfortable with this." Then what?

The younger you are, the easier it is to adjust. If I wanted to be a certified public accountant one day and a fireman the next, I could adjust at will, every day, several times a day if I wanted to as a child. But, get to college, name a major, don't really like it, and now switch majors—still doable. Many people change majors; it's just a bit more hassle. Start a new job right out of college, hate it, change jobs in the first year—that's fairly easy to do. Get married, have two kids, buy a huge house, build some credit card debt, work ten plus years for the same place—how easy is it now? Not very.

So we spend our lives making plans, we adjust as we go, but the older we get, the more set in our ways we become. We develop grooves. The more we hang inside the grooves, the deeper they get. Ever try to pull a vehicle out of grooves deeply cut into a road? It's not easy, and there will be bumps along the way.

Sometimes, the grooves were started by decisions we made years ago that no longer serve us. You got a job, fell in love, got married, and you bought a house. Fifteen years later, is it still the job you want? Maybe you didn't even want it back then! It's just what you fell into, and you never left. Would this be the job you'd try to get if you were looking to get a job today? If not, why stay? Money? Security? Insurance? What is the internal cost of working eight hours a day at a job you don't like just for the money? It's extensive.

What about your marriage? Would you do it again? Is this the person you would pick out of a crowd and fall in love with all over again like you did when you first met? Or are you just tolerating each other for the kid's sake? Or convenience? People change. Staying in a bad relationship can wreak havoc on your soul as well.

What about your stuff? Your house, your car, your boat, your clothes, your tinker toy collection—are you holding on to things that no longer serve you? Pants from when your waistline was four inches smaller than it is now because "someday" I'll fit into them again? Someday, even though they've been on the shelf for over five years.

We tend to hang on to things we get comfortable with without spending a lot of time re-examining if the decisions we made years ago still serve us. We forget we have options. What if you started looking for a different job just to see what's out there? Maybe there's a job you'd really like that pays more and has better benefits than what you have now. Well, you'll miss it if you're not looking. You can't hit a target you never hung on the wall.

What about your relationship? If it isn't what you'd like it to be, then you have two choices—actually three. One is to live with it as it is because it's the easiest—probably the default setting here. Two is to work on the relationship. See if you can find the spark that brought you together in the first place. Three is to realize you've grown apart and move on. Moving on from a relationship, especially one that has become abusive, can be an extremely dangerous and scary thing to do. There are organizations that help in such situations. Freedom is on the other side of fear. That's easy to say, but very tough to do. Would you want to know if the person you're in a relationship with has fallen out of love with you, or would you rather they just hung in there out of comfort and duty? A bad home life affects everything else in life.

And why hang on to things that have outlived their usefulness? The boat you haven't used in two years. The cottage you go to twice every summer. The land you were going to build on twenty-three years ago—sell it, give it away, move on. I'm not good at this one myself, so in trying to change my own thinking, maybe I can throw some pants in the Goodwill pile when I get home.

Our lives are what we make them to be. We have choices. Those choices determine our happiness. Happy people tend to be grateful people. They look for love. They hang out with other happy people. They seek God in their lives. This is an upward path. A job you hate, a bad home life, junk all over your yard and home—these will keep you down. You get one life and infinite options. Adjust as necessary.

priorities

04/21/2018

WHEN I GOT TO FLORIDA TO WRITE THIS BOOK, I
THOUGHT I'D WRITE IN THE MORNING A LOT, maybe into
the afternoon. By dinner I'd be free to do whatever else needed to be
done. Groceries, laundry, dishes, etc. I also figured I'd write from Monday
through Friday, taking off Saturdays and Sundays if I got enough done
during the week. I would then use the weekends to explore. Writing fifteen easy-to-read twenty-minute chapters in three weeks was my loose
goal—one chapter a day, five days a week, with two days off or as backup
in case or writer's block. This, of course, is totally not what happened.

First off, I had no idea what I was bringing with me emotionally. I worked
long, hard hours leading up to this trip to allow me to block three weeks
off my schedule. As it is, I work a lot, but the month leading up to Florida
was busier than I've ever been. I work almost every Saturday, so I packed
my bags on a Saturday after work and flew out early Sunday morning.

Sunday was a day of travel. I got in early, got situated mid-afternoon, and
went to explore a bit that night.

Monday was day number one of writing—and an emotional meltdown. Many tears were shed. Not just this day, but over the course of the next three days. I experienced a serious release that needed to take place to open a channel for the writing to occur. But, why? Where was this coming from?

Today is the thirteenth full day of my nineteen-day book writing expedition. Looking back now, I can see that before I left, my priorities were a mess. I hate getting up early and rushing, but that's what I had done back home almost every day. I like working out later in the day, but all my workouts had been scheduled in the morning. I don't like getting behind on anything, but I had so much business that we were always behind. I love to read, but I had little time for that, and I never meditated. I didn't do yoga. Basically, by far, my number one priority was my job. I worked every night, Monday through Thursday, and every Saturday. Only Sundays off. For years. At one point I really loved my job, but that love wears thin with overuse. It had left very little time for anything else. I had no idea how tense I was—until I got to Florida.

In Florida, I went to bed when I was tired. I got out of bed when I woke up naturally. I ate when I got hungry. I didn't keep any "bad" food in the house. I wrote when I felt like it, read when I felt like it, and meditated every day when I felt like it. I had a few things I wanted to do. –Michael Singer, author of *The Untethered Soul* and *The Surrender Experiment*, gave talks every Monday and Thursday night and Sunday mornings. I went to all of those. I started to discover that as much as I love solitude—and I love being alone maybe because I was an only child—I also need human interaction. I had no TV. No stereo. It was very quiet. Sounds awesome, right? And it was...for a few days. Then I wanted noise. I wanted to see people. Have a conversation. So I started planning at least one excursion per day to get me out and about. Massages, acupuncture, checking out interesting shops in the area, restaurants, anything where I'd get a little human interaction. I needed it daily.

I also found I couldn't just sit and write, get a massage, go to the store, and do nothing else physically. Since I didn't have gym access, I got back into running on a daily basis, which was tough at first, but it became a bit of a "moving meditation" for me. I went through chapter ideas in my head. Eventually, I found that running just before the sun went down was my favorite. A little statue of Buddha sat at the end of the road where stayed, so the final leg of the run was always "run to Buddha." I'd get to the end, hold my right hand on his head and meditate a while. Then I'd switch to my left hand, two taps on Buddha's belly, and that was my day.

I absolutely loved my time in Florida. But I had no one to share it with. Even my dog wasn't with me. I can get human interaction at the grocery store, but I can't get love. And, by nobody else's fault but my own, my life had a severe love deficiency because I wasn't making it a priority.

Have you ever seen a sign that read, "Work is love"? No? How about, "God is love"?

I meditated every day that I was in Florida. It was a priority for me. I also read every day as well. My normal journaling is three pages a day, the first couple days in Florida were six pages plus. I wrote every day. I ran every day. I realized I also needed to get yoga into my life as well. More than one person has since told me they can feel the change in me. This trip will end soon, though. And then what?

I hope to take this experience back with me and make some changes to my schedule once I got back to allow me the time I need for recharging and reflection. But it's really so much more than that. How did I ever forget to make love a priority? I guess I thought it was…until I got to Florida and saw the release of sadness that came out of me. That didn't say to me, "Everything is alright." It said, "You need help." Help, in my case, came from removing the things that stopped me from allowing more love to flow into my life. Everything is possible. Schedules can be altered. We all have time for whatever we want to have time for; sometimes, we just forget we have control, and we get out of sync with our highest ideals.

If you can take three weeks off and seclude yourself in the woods of Florida, I highly recommend it. If not, take a personal day and look at everything. What are your priorities? What would you like them to be? Only one person can make sure you're living life the way you want to live it. Get your priorities in order. Take back the love.

love

04/23/2018

LET'S SAY I BUILT A MACHINE CALLED THE "LOVE-O-ME-TER" that when used could give you a rating from one to ten of where you are in the love continuum—ten being the highest, basically God consciousness, a fully enlightened being; zero being nothing but darkness, like a house with all the windows shuttered, no light at all, no love. Where would you land on the love continuum if we hooked you up to the "love-o-meter"? Three? Five? Seven? Seven would be fairly high. Think about everything you do all day long. How much is really done with love in your heart? How easy would it be to get you upset? We have an ocean of love inside us if we would just seek it, yet we're getting angry because the store is out of our favorite bread, or we can't find a parking spot, or the dog peed on the new carpet. What does it matter?

If we look at how everything is on earth today, we see it all as separate. Separate people driving separate cars to separate jobs with separate companies in separate cities, states, countries, planets, galaxies, and so on. This separation occurs in our mind. It's man-made. From that belief, when held as reality, comes all our problems with finding more love in our lives. Because when we view everything as separate, we create a mentality within ourselves that says, "I will be happy if…" If I get either what

I want or avoid what I don't want. The love becomes conditional. Buddha said, "The root of all suffering is desire." If we predicate our love on a specific outcome, then we are setting ourselves up for disappointment.

If we'd like to get to ten on the love spectrum, then we need to tap into the love already inside us, which we just haven't looked for yet. It's an unconditional love, and it flows through everything. Yes, everything—you, the chair, your car, the guy you can't stand at work, lizards, spiders, rocks—everything.

Do you believe that God is omnipresent? If God is everywhere, then where is he not? Of course, God is everywhere in everything always. So why can't we see that? Because we're seeing with our minds, not our souls.

When you're in love with another person, certain traits about that person make him or her endearing to you. Let's say it's their laugh. When they laugh, your heart melts and you think, "I just love their laugh," and you can feel that love in your heart. You can look at each other and have one of those "moments in time" when you connect without using any words—the love is so strong.

When we're in love with another person, there will also be things about that person we can't stand. Let's say they crack their knuckles. Every time they crack their knuckles, it's like fingers on a chalkboard—your mind goes crazy, anger wells up, and you wonder what you ever saw in this person. Right? There are things they'll do that you won't enjoy.

Now let's back up to that awesome "moment in time" we were having. Your partner was laughing, love welled up inside of you, our eyes connected—and they cracked their knuckles. The moment is over. The love is lost. Conditional love changes with conditions. Change the conditions, change the love.

If we look deeper, we'll see that everything is made up of energy. At a subatomic level, everything we think is solid—isn't. It's all energy, including us. Scientists study these things, and I do not claim to know anything at all about quantum physics, but I do believe that what they've found is that everything we see as separate, when reduced to infinitesimal levels, is made up of energy. The energy is always moving and changing, but everything is one. It's that energy that is unconditional love, that flows through everything, that we know as God, that will make all the difference for us. Because once you see that, how can you look at anyone or anything without love? It's all you; you are it, and there are no expectations or conditions to be met. And it flows through everything, not only in this world, but all planets in all galaxies in the entire universe. There is an entire universe of unconditional love inside of you if you just look within and get in touch with it.

Very few of us will ever get to ten on the "love-o-meter," but it's hard to move up the scale when we temper our love with conditions. Lasting change is made when we know and see the power that unconditional love brings to our lives. It's available to all. No purchase necessary. You are already the owner of the universe of love.

balance

04/23/2018

BALANCE IS A TOPIC I STRUGGLE WITH in all areas of life, including the physical. I will never walk a tight rope, and I'm totally fine with that. I'm not going to win any balance beam competitions either. I know that if I worked on it, then I would get better than I am now, though. This works the same with balance in our emotional and work-home lives as well.

As a generally obsessive-compulsive person, I often tend to be "all in" or "out." The part of me that goes "all in," well, that's also the part that wants to be number one. I don't want to just get good at it; I want to know everything about it and outwork or outperform everyone. No matter what. The subtitle to this book is "overcoming our addiction to ego"—well, here's where my ego roars up and takes action. I will be the number one salesman. I will run farther, faster than anyone in my age group. I will buy the coolest guitars ever made. If I want it, I'm gonna get it. I have the coolest stuff. I win all the awards. You can't beat me. Ugh! So much of my life has been dominated by this part of me. It's the part that makes me work ridiculously long hours. I wear a suit at work, and some people swear I have a different aura when I'm in work mode. This Dave is often referred to as "Suit Dave." This Dave gets things done. He's focused, driven, and motivated.

Then there's "Hoodie Dave," who likes to read and meditate. Hoodie Dave is the author of this book. I had never spent so much extended time with Hoodie Dave—this is my fifteenth full day in Florida today. Hoodie Dave is awesome. He works at a much slower pace than Suit Dave. He smiles more. He looks for love in everyone and everything, has a great sense of humor, and loves music.

Hoodie Dave went to Woodstock.

Suit Dave voted for Nixon.

You get the picture. It's not like these two parts of me are mutually exclusive. Suit Dave has a good sense of humor and smiles now and then, and Hoodie Dave can be curmudgeon. But to exist in the world, we have to learn how to have balance. If we overdo in one area, then by default, we will overlook a different area of our lives. There's a self-assessment called the "wheel of life," which you can find online. You can rate yourself in different categories like career, finance, health, family, friends, romance, spirituality, and so on. Most of us have areas on which we're over concentrating and other areas we're overlooking.

At times, however, we have to focus on one area or another for a while. For example, if you're starting a new business, that endeavor will take up more of your time. If you have a new baby, then family becomes the priority. If you have physical issues, then caring for your health becomes the major player. Your focus changes constantly.

Sometimes, we forget to rethink and revise our selections, though. For example, let's say you opened a new restaurant and have worked sixty to eighty hours a week getting it going. Now it's one of the most popular restaurants in town. You have a manager you trust, and ten years have passed—but you're still working sixty to eighty hours a week. Is that focus on your business really necessary? It used to be, but could you rethink your priorities now and spend more time with family and friends?

Trying to balance the wheel of life is a tricky proposition. It's like every category that makes up our lives is a plate we're spinning on a stick, and if we don't pay attention to them all, then something is going to hit the floor. And if we focus on only one or two, well, then we stand to lose most of them. It pays to know which areas are the most important to us and make sure those plates never hit the floor. Health. Spirituality. Family. Can we really afford any loss? Any time we focus on only one or two areas, we will have casualties elsewhere. Pay attention and keep those plates in motion. With a little focus, it is possible to keep them all going forever without a loss.

CHAPTER 17

the bottom line

04/24/2018

HUMANS HAVE BODIES. Our bodies are basically our "packaging." Who we are is held within the body. With all the bodies that have ever come before us and all the bodies that will come after, there will never be a body exactly like the one we were born with. Some people get a normal, healthy body. Others get defects right out the gate. Whatever body you have, it is the vehicle you get to work with, and it's up to us to take care of our body once we're in it. Some people with perfectly fine bodies will abuse them until they start to fail. Others who have major defects to overcome will not let their bodies deter them—Helen Keller and Stephen Hawking, for example. It's much like joining the military and being issued one uniform only. That's it. If the clothes don't quite fit right, if the shoes are too tight—tough. No returns. You get one uniform—the one you have. Wash it and care for it, and it will last and look good. Let it get stinky and dirty, and people won't want to be near you. What you do after you get your body is up to you.

Inside this body is where we live. We control the body for the most part. We have a mind and a soul—previously called the "fast mind" and "slow mind," respectively. And both dwell inside the body. The health of the body can affect the health of the mind and vice versa, as discussed previously. The soul stands alone and is not affected by any physical or mental misgivings; it is forever. It is where we truly reside, watching as our minds and bodies act out our lives.

Basically, we are issued this rather incredible device called a body that allows us to get around in the world, to do things, to see, hear, taste and feel. The body is this fantastic vehicle we've been given, and we also have been given the choice to take care of it as we see fit.

Inside this vehicle it comes equipped with the world's best and finest supercomputer ever built—our minds. Our minds are incredible. They can store, analyze, think and relate. They can overcome tremendous adversities and obstacles, invent things and split the atom. Whatever we have created in civilization—homes, cars, rocket ships, Cheerios, books, everything—was developed using this incredible gift we've been given, the mind.

At birth we got a body and a mind capable of doing whatever we decide we want to do with them. By the way, who is it that receives these gifts? The essence of who we truly are—the soul, the part we can only find by looking within—receives the gifts. Our bodies and minds do not define us. They are basically the car and computer we got at birth to play with however we want.

So what do we do with these gifts? We eat too much. We smoke too much. We drink too much. We don't get enough rest. We create too much stress. We basically give them as much abuse as we can and see what they can handle. A car will stop running if not taken care of properly, which would also shut down the computer. The computer can only work with the information it's been given. If the computer malfunctions, the car can malfunction. They're interconnected. Sometimes we're just so focused on the cool stuff we get to use we forget about who it is that uses it.

A computer uses only the data it's been programmed with. Bad data equals bad results. The computers we are born with (our minds) are completely blank. All the data is created by us only, nobody else. Then we infuse that data with emotion—both good and bad. The really good and really bad data gets stuck at the forefront of our memory banks. Most data just flies right through without really sticking. Do you remember what you ate for dinner thirty-seven days ago? Probably not, unless it was your birthday, there was a big party, everyone was there, and they made your favorite meal. Or that was the night your wife asked you for a divorce—right there in the restaurant on your birthday. Either way, good or bad, those memories will "stick." Eventually, they start to clog up the memory bank. So what do we do? We put the computer on "auto-pilot" and walk away…from our lives.

The computer is now making decisions for us. It does this by looking at all past experiences that are stuck in the memory bank, trying to re-create the good ones while avoiding the bad ones. This is all the data it has to go by. So if we had an Uncle Ed who gave us noogies—who likes getting noogies?—those memories get stored. Years later, we're dating someone, and at a holiday gathering they excitedly introduce you to their "Uncle Ed", and the computer goes nuts—bells, whistles, alarms—"Uncle Ed" is bad; he gives you noogies! You become very uncomfortable, even though your Uncle Ed died twenty years ago.

The opposite is also true. Your Aunt Mary always made brownies for you and gave you a dollar every time you visited her. You loved Aunt Mary. During move-in day of your freshman year of college, you're introduced to your roommate's Aunt Mary. Instantly, you like her based on information that is fifteen years old and faulty.

The mind will flip-flop and vacillate back and forth as well. It's extremely wishy-washy. You meet this new Aunt Mary, you like her right away, and she offers you brownies! Oh, man! What a great deal this is. Then she excuses herself to go outside and smoke a cigarette. Well, your Aunt Mary hated smoking, and you don't like it either. Maybe this Aunt Mary isn't all she's cracked up to be.

You can see how one piece of new information can throw the whole network of thoughts for a loop when you let thoughts determine the course of your life. There will be upset. There will be suffering. Left unchecked, the mind always makes a mess of things.

In the meantime, behind it all, the real you watches everything unfold. It watches you get upset, watches you fall in love, watches you question yourself, and watches you worry. It watches you let things that happened forty years ago affect your thoughts today. Why doesn't it help?

It doesn't help because you never looked, you never cared, you never asked. When things started going badly, your mind threw your hands up to the sky and you shouted, "Please God, help me!", to a God that was already inside of you. The self, the soul, is an ocean of loving energy and it's accessible to everyone, but we have to look within. And when we do, amazing things begin to happen.

All those "stuck" memories won't seem so sticky anymore. Once you're in touch with that part of you that watches, you'll be able to "unstick" them. This usually happens a little at a time. Eventually, you'll just go through life enjoying the experiences without any expectations on outcome. When you get to the point where you have no more "stuck" memories, and live only from the part of you that watches—this is what is known as enlightenment.

The "watcher" is one with everything. What is there to desire if everything is you? How can you see the world with anything but love? You become centered. If and when the mind wants to freak out and stick a memory in the forefront of your memory bank, you step back and relax. Everything is awesome every second of every day. Happiness is not determined by getting your way. It is the way.

You have amazing, fantastic and beautiful tools to use. They weren't meant to build a network of insecurity and despair. Yet this is where so many of us go.

The way out is within. You were born with everything you need to be free. You just haven't been looking for it in the right place. Know yourself as the one who watches. Step into the calm, the love, the one that is all. Then live from there.

epilogue
04/26/2018

I did it! The book won't be as large as I had hoped, but I did it. Wow. I wrote my book, which you now hold in your hands. And in the process, I might have changed my life forever once again. Today is my eighteenth full day in Florida. I have one full day left here, then I fly back to Wisconsin on Saturday. As I wrote, I never looked back to see what I had written on the prior day(s). I didn't have time, really. I just went on to the next thing. I had thirty-five index cards with chapter titles on them and just pulled out the ones I felt like writing about on any given day. Of the thirty-five cards, seventeen made it into this book. I never got stuck. I wrote only when I felt like it, and it never felt forced. For seven years I thought about writing this book, and in eighteen days I did it. Unreal. I was in no way prepared for what this experience turned out to be like. It is one of the best things I've ever done for myself.

First came the emotional release, and it was substantial. It was just like the early days of alcohol and drug counseling. And with it came this realization: I've been addicted to my ego, and I just entered recovery. Thus, the book's subtitle "Overcoming our addiction to ego."

Then there were the talks at the Temple of the Universe. As of this writing, I've seen Michael Singer speak seven times and give seven different talks, with no notes. I'm seeing him again tonight. For free. A fantastic speaker and a brilliant mind. One of the talks was quite possibly the best spiritual talk I've ever heard. He nailed it. Even people who have been coming to his talks for years said it was special. These talks helped me get clear on a lot of things I wrote about in this book.

There was silence. No TV. No stereo—except when driving. Very little human interaction—I found out how important human interaction is. So I set at least one excursion outside my Airbnb a day, so I could interact with other humans.

For the first time in a long time, after the emotional release, I felt peace. Peace that I haven't felt for many years, and I realized this shouldn't be something I feel every twenty to thirty years. It should truly be a way of life.

I engaged in the many daily rituals that I had always thought were important but didn't do at home. I meditated. I ran when it wasn't pouring rain. I did yoga. I got massages and acupuncture. I read a lot. I wrote. I ate well and kept portion sizes reasonable.

I released a lot of blockages I had built up over my life that didn't allow love to flow as freely as it should. I had many moments when I was overcome with love while in Florida. Weird moments, too—like when having lunch or driving in the car. I would just get overwhelmed with how crazy amazing everything is, and love would just flow through me.

I couldn't have asked for a better place to stay. You take a chance on Airbnb, especially on a three-week stay, and my God, I'd buy this place if it were for sale. I so love it here. It feels like home. I'll always remember it—I think I'll come back often—because I changed my life here. I took eighteen days off, and I'll never be the same.

Everything fell into place. The whole thing was crazy—who I met, who they knew, where they sent me. I found great restaurants, I met some great local coworkers of mine, all the fitness and health people I met were fantastic. I didn't have a single bad experience. I thank many of them in the special thank yous section at the back of this book.

My body and mind haven't felt this good in a long, long time. Who knew all it took was three weeks in the woods in Florida?

I gave myself nineteen days to write a book. I had visions of how it would go. I chose instead to follow the path I was given rather than the one I had created. The book is now completed on this, the eighteenth day. Tomorrow I rest. Saturday, I go home a much different person than the one who came here three weeks ago.

This was a retreat. I retreated into God's arms, and He helped me remember what love feels like.

Thanks for walking these pages with me as I try to figure it all out.

Whoever you are, wherever you are, I love you.

We are one.

David Geschke
Horsepower Farms "Treehouse"
High Springs, Florida
April 26th, 2018

very
special thank yous
to the following people and organizations

Temple Of The Universe
Hosts Michael Singer's talks
Monday and Thursday 8:15pm • Sunday 9:30am
www.tou.org

Mike and Judi Kearney, hosts
Horsepower Farms "Treehouse"
www.airbnb.com/rooms/151509?s=51

Bambi's Country Farm Market
Great vegetarian and vegan options
www.bambisfarm.com

Nancy Lavin Linkous, Licensed Massage Therapist
Back In Balance Natural Health Care
www.highspringsbackinbalance.com

Hamilton Rotte, Acupuncturist
The Healing House of Alachua
www.healinghousealachua.com

Lauren Wilsman, Private Yoga Instructor
Zen Vibe Yoga
www.zenvibeyoga.com

48988613R00050

Made in the USA
Columbia, SC
18 January 2019